Homeland Operations

Air Force Doctrine Document 3-27
23 April 2013

This document complements related discussion found in Joint Publications (JP) 3-27, *Homeland Defense*, and 3-28, *Civil Support*.

BY ORDER OF THE
SECRETARY OF THE AIR FORCE

AIR FORCE DOCTRINE DOCUMENT 3-27
23 APRIL 2013

SUMMARY OF CHANGES

This revision significantly updates the previous Air Force Doctrine Document (AFDD) 3-27, *Homeland Operations*.

Chapter 1 has been revised to more fully define the scope of homeland operations. It incorporates updated national guidance published since the previous edition. Chapter 2 more clearly defines command relationships and introduces the concept of dual status commanders. Chapters 3 and 4 have been substantially updated to reflect recent operations and guidance. Appendix C has been removed, with material incorporated into Chapter 4.

See AFI 10-1301, *Air Force Doctrine*, for procedures on recommending changes to this publication.

Supersedes: AFDD 3-27, 21 Mar 2006
OPR: LeMay Center/DDS
Certified by: LeMay Center/DD (Col Todd C. Westhauser)
Pages: 58
Accessibility: Available on the e-publishing website at www.e-publishing.af.mil for downloading
Releasability: There are no releasability restrictions on this publication
Approved by: WALTER D. GIVHAN, Major General, USAF
        Commander, LeMay Center for Doctrine Development and Education

FOREWORD

The attacks of 11 September 2001 served as a stark reminder of the importance of homeland operations. The defense of America's territory and air sovereignty quickly returned to the forefront of national discourse. Since 9/11, we have also seen the destructive power of nature in the form of Hurricane Katrina, many devastating tornadoes, and numerous wildfires throughout the country.

AFDD 3-27 describes how our Air Force organizes and employs airpower in the homeland, whether in a Federal or State capacity. It focuses on providing support to civilian authorities in a variety of operations, from defense of the homeland to support for natural disasters. AFDD 3-27 represents our best practices for dealing with the complexities and special considerations encountered with the interagency process for conducting homeland operations.

WALTER D. GIVHAN
Major General, USAF
Commander, LeMay Center for Doctrine
Development and Education

TABLE OF CONTENTS

PREFACE

Air Force Doctrine Document (AFDD) 3-27, *Homeland Operations*, establishes doctrinal guidance for Air Force operations in the United States (US) and its territories. It presents best practices and experiences that will help Airmen fully integrate into joint operations securing the homeland.

Chapter 1, *Fundamentals*, establishes the nature and definition of homeland operations. It highlights relevant national policy and the role of the Air Force in securing national objectives.

Chapter 2, *Command and Organization*, discusses how the Air Force presents forces to homeland operations. It covers the full range of potential command structures and command relationships.

Chapter 3, *Planning, Execution, and Assessment*, provides sample mission sets for homeland operations. Planning considerations for these various missions are presented, as are the actions required to execute as appropriate.

Chapter 4, *Emergency Preparedness*, looks at how the Air Force total force prepares for various emergencies (natural or man-made). It details how each level of planning (local through federal) readies Air Force personnel and capabilities to respond in time of need.

Appendix A, *National Policy and Law*, serves as a quick-reference guide to a variety of national policy sources, as well as some of the legal limitations placed on military forces working within US territory. Appendix B, *Notional Sequence for Defense Support of Civil Authorities*, provides a notional flow of how Air Force personnel and capabilities would be fielded in support of homeland operations.

The doctrine in this document is authoritative, but not directive and requires judgment in application. Therefore, commanders should consider the contents of this AFDD and the particular situation when accomplishing their missions. Airmen should read it, discuss it, and practice it.

Nearly every Airman, regardless of primary mission or component, could be called upon to support homeland operations. As such, this document applies to all Airmen.

CHAPTER ONE

FUNDAMENTALS

We will not apologize for our way of life, nor will we waver in its defense. And for those who seek to advance their aims by inducing terror and slaughtering innocents, we say to you now that our spirit is stronger and cannot be broken—you cannot outlast us, and we will defeat you.

—**President Barack Obama, Inaugural Address. January 20. 2009**

BOUNDING HOMELAND OPERATIONS

The greatest responsibility of the federal government is protecting the American people.[1] As such, great emphasis is placed on homeland security—"a concerted national effort to prevent terrorist attacks within the US; reduce America's vulnerability to terrorism, major disasters, and other emergencies; and minimize the damage and recover from attacks, major disasters, and other emergencies that do occur."[2] The Department of Defense (DOD) contributes to this aspect of national security by conducting homeland defense (HD), defense support of civil authorities (DSCA), and emergency preparedness (EP).

For the Air Force, homeland operations is the umbrella construct through which it supports HD, DSCA, and EP. It incorporates all operations planning and execution designed to detect, preempt, respond to, mitigate, and recover from the full spectrum of incidents and threats to the homeland, whether man-made or natural. The geographic homeland boundaries include the 50 states, four territories, and

Operating within the homeland is not the same as homeland operations. Though operating within the same geographic area of responsibility, Service Department activities undertaken to accomplish the Title 10, U.S. Code (U.S.C.), and responsibilities to organize, train and equip forces are not considered within the purview of the homeland operations construct.

---

[1] *National Security Strategy*, May 2010.
[2] *National Strategy for Homeland Security*, October 2007.

numerous island possessions.[3] The US also enjoys exclusive sovereignty 12 nautical miles out to sea and exercises responsibilities extending 200 nautical miles from the coast.[4]

In summary, security of the homeland is a national objective to protect people and territories.[5] The Air Force supports this objective via homeland operations: HD, DSCA, and EP. Figure 1.1 provides a graphic depiction of the homeland operations construct.

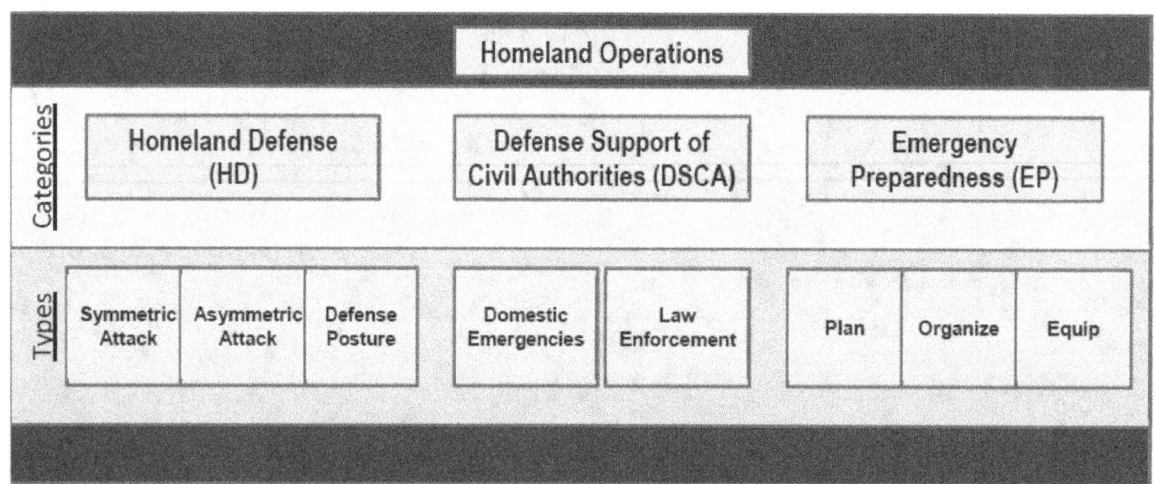

Figure 1.1. Homeland Operations Construct

A key distinction between HD and DSCA is that in HD, DOD is the lead federal agency (LFA), while in DSCA, another federal organization is the LFA, with DOD acting in support (see figure 1.2).[6]

Homeland Defense

HD is defined as "the protection of US sovereignty, territory, domestic population, and critical defense infrastructure against external threats and aggression or other threats as directed by the President."[7]

For the Air Force, HD operations involve significant counterair emphasis and may be supported by preemptive actions through global strike operations against threats to the US homeland or US forces and installations throughout the world. In addition, forces

---

[3] The territories and insular possessions of the United States are enumerated in Title 48, U.S. Code (U.S.C).
[4] The 1982 United Nations Convention on the Law of the Sea, to which the United States is a signatory, establishes the 12 nautical mile limit for territorial waters and the 200 nautical mile limit for an exclusive economic zone.
[5] *National Security Strategy*, May 2010.
[6] Joint Publication (JP) 3-27, *Homeland Defense*, 12 July 2007, and JP 3-28, *Civil Support*, 14 Sept 2007.
[7] JP 3-27.

(conventional and special operations) operating to locate, characterize, and secure weapons of mass destruction (WMD) provide another option to defend and respond against WMD attacks or threats.[8] Cyber defense capabilities are continuing to develop, and may also be employed to support and defend US assets.

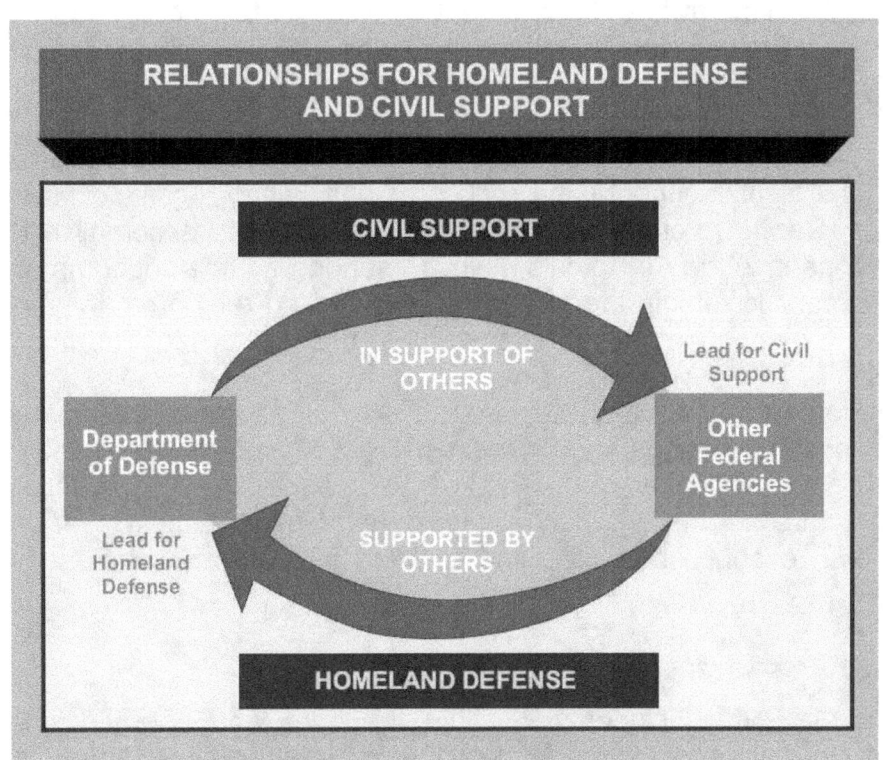

Figure 1.2. Relationships for HD and Civil Support (DSCA) (from JP 3-28)

Defense Support of Civil Authorities

DSCA, often referred to as civil support, is defined as support provided "by US Federal military forces, DOD civilians, DOD contract personnel, DOD component assets, and National Guard forces (when the Secretary of Defense, in coordination wtitht he governors of the affected states, elects and requests to use those forces in Title 32, U.S.C., status) in response to requests for assistance from civil authorities, for domestic emergencies, law enforcement support, and other domestic activities, or from qualifying entities for special events."[9] It includes military assistance for civil law enforcement operations in very limited circumstances. For example, DSCA missions can include support to the Department of Justice (DOJ) in preventing or defeating terrorist attacks, or aiding local agency response to natural disasters, among others.[10] In all these missions, various federal, state, or local civilian agencies are responsible for the management of the particular incident.

---

[8] JP 3-40, Combating WMD, 10 June 2009.
[9] DOD Directive (DODD) 3025.18, *Defense Support of Civil Authorities (DSCA)*.
[10] JP 3-41, *Chemical, Biological, Radiological, and Nuclear Consequence Management*, 21 June 2012.

DOD operations within the US are governed by law, including the Posse Comitatus Act (PCA), that prohibits use of the military forces in Title 10 status for law enforcement purposes, except as authorized by Congress and the US Constitution. This PCA restriction does not apply to ANG forces in state status. For DSCA, the Air Force's involvement is supportive, and dependent on a request to the DOD from the designated lead agency. Planning considerations, HD and DSCA missions are discussed more thoroughly in Chapter 3.

Many of the same forces needed to support military operations overseas and at home may be highly sought by the civil community when a crisis occurs. The Secretary of Defense (SecDef) determines the degree of DSCA to accomplish the mission that does not jeopardize the Air Force's ability to support combatant commanders (CCDRs). Combat operations remain the highest priority for the Air Force; these operations take precedence over noncombat operations unless directed by higher authority.

Air Force organizations that provide support for domestic emergencies use the Air Force incident management system (AFIMS) structure to comply with Homeland Security Presidential Directive (HSPD) 5, *Management of Domestic Incidents*. The AFIMS structure mirrors the national incident management system (NIMS) structure used by civil response agencies and outlined in the National Response Framework (NRF).[11]

Emergency Preparedness

The Air Force includes EP within the homeland operations umbrella. EP is defined as "the measures taken in advance of an emergency to reduce the loss of life and property, and to protect a nation's institutions from all types of hazards through a comprehensive emergency management program of preparedness, mitigation, response and recovery."[12]

Homeland operations routinely involve a unique collaboration between federal, state, local, and tribal agencies, which present a number of challenges. These agencies may have different resources, levels of experience, and legal considerations. Regional partnerships may be established that should be considered. For more about EP missions and planning considerations, see Chapter 4.

NATIONAL POLICY FOR HOMELAND SECURITY

As with any Air Force mission, the Service role in homeland operations is directed and guided by national policy. The National Security Strategy (NSS) provides the overarching national guidance for providing a safe and secure environment for the American people. It lists national level priorities in pursuit of US security objectives. Two

---

[11] For detailed information, see Air Force Instruction (AFI) 10-2501, *Air Force Emergency Management Program Planning and Operations.*
[12] JP 1-02, *Department of Defense Dictionary of Military and Associated Terms.*

major documents further detail the DOD role in homeland operations: the NRF and the National Strategy for Homeland Security (NSHS).

National Response Framework

The NRF is a guide to how the Nation conducts all-hazards response. It is built upon scalable, flexible, and adaptable coordinating structures to align key roles and responsibilities across the Nation. It describes specific authorities and best practices for managing incidents that range from the serious but purely local, to large-scale terrorist attacks or catastrophic natural disasters.

The term "response" as used in the NRF includes immediate actions to save lives, protect property and the environment, and meet basic human needs. Response also includes the execution of emergency plans and actions to support short-term recovery. The NRF is always in effect, and elements can be implemented as needed on a flexible, scalable basis to improve response.

It is written especially for government executives, private sector and nongovernmental organization leaders, and emergency management practitioners. First, it is addressed to senior elected and appointed leaders, such as federal department or agency heads, state governors, mayors, tribal leaders, and city or county officials—those who have a responsibility to provide for effective response. For the nation to be prepared for any and all hazards, its leaders should have a baseline familiarity with the concepts and mechanics of the NRF.

The NRF defines the principles, roles, and structures that organize how the US responds as a nation.[13] The NRF:

- Describes how communities, tribes, states, the federal government, private sectors, and nongovernmental partners work together to coordinate national response.

- Describes specific authorities and best practices for managing incidents.

- Builds upon the NIMS, which provides a consistent template for managing incidents.

Dealing with the immediate consequences of a catastrophic incident is a local responsibility. State or federal involvement is usually contingent on a request for support from the local authorities. Terrorist incidents, however, such as 9/11 or those preceded by substantial threat warning, may involve the overlapping authorities of local, state, and federal agencies. Each of these agencies has a role in data collection, analysis, threat response, and response and recovery. While every attempt is made to maintain local and state control of domestic incidents, attacks and disasters deemed of significance to national security may be managed under federal jurisdiction.

---

[13] HSPD-5 directed the establishment of the National Response Plan (NRP). The NRP emphasized a seamless, nationally integrated response rather than a fragmented response effort. The NRP has since been updated and replaced by the NRF, effective March 22, 2008.

This federal involvement has the potential for conflict, with local authorities in the lead for managing the consequences of an event, while federal authorities lead the effort when national security is at stake. The numerous local, state, and federal agencies that may participate in homeland operations, each with a differing chain of command, can complicate response efforts. By establishing an integrated response capability to support these efforts, the DOD and the Air Force are capable of supporting any mission called upon to perform.

National Strategy For Homeland Security

The NSHS is designed to mobilize and organize the nation to secure the US homeland from terrorist attacks. The strategic objectives of homeland security and how the Air Force supports them are to:[14]

- ✪ **Prevent and disrupt terrorist attacks.** To prevent attacks against the US, Air Force forces deter, detect, predict, plan for, and preempt threats to the homeland. Air Force operations can prevent attack through early warning and military operations overseas.

- ✪ **Protect the American people, critical infrastructure, and key resources**. Air Force operations can reduce America's vulnerability to terrorist attacks by air patrols over specific locations or resources. Other examples are military support to law enforcement (MSLE) during special events or national special security events (NSSE) such as the Olympics, the Super Bowl, and Presidential movements. In addition, the Air Force places special emphasis on securing and safeguarding stockpiles of nuclear and conventional weapons and associated facilities, whether operationally deployed, in storage, in transit, or awaiting disposal.

- ✪ **Respond to and recover from incidents that do occur.** Through DSCA, Air Force forces respond with such resources as rapidly deployable medical capabilities and civil engineer expertise as key contributors. The Air Force has the ability to provide logistics at all levels of operation, from bare base to main operating base support.

- ✪ **Continue to strengthen the foundation to ensure long-term success.** Joint planning and mutual training exercises with civil authorities well before an incident occurs reduce America's vulnerability and provide force protection for Air Force forces.

AIR FORCE SUPPORT FOR THE HOMELAND SECURITY MISSION OF THE DOD

Within the US, the NSHS envisions circumstances under which the DOD and therefore the Air Force would be involved in improving security at home. Specific instances where the Air Force could play a key role include:

---

[14] *National Strategy for Homeland Security*, October 2007.

- Air surveillance, aerospace control alert, and direct air defense operations to defend US citizens and territory. The extraordinary events of 9/11 increased steady-state air defense operations, which have since been normalized and now adjust as needed to known and perceived threats.

- Cyberspace defense. Because our nation has become more dependent on information technology, defense of the cyberspace domain has become more critical. The Air Force plays an indispensable role in this effort.

- Quick response in support of civilian agencies by providing forces and capabilities during an emergency such as an attack or natural disaster.

- Participation in "limited scope" missions where other agencies have primary responsibility for security such as at NSSE like the Olympics or the State of the Union Address.

- Support to a joint task force (JTF) or federal coordinating officer (FCO) under DSCA as a designated base support installation. Support may include use of the installation infrastructure, personnel, equipment, and ancillary resources.

All requests from civilian agencies for DOD assistance, except those provided under mutual aid agreements or immediate response authority, flow through the Joint Staff's Joint Director of Military Support (JDOMS). JDOMS is the clearinghouse for accepting interagency mission assignments. JDOMS routes their recommendation to the Chairman of the Joint Chiefs of Staff for SecDef approval.

Regular Air Force Airmen and activated Reservists are always under the command of military commanders up through the SecDef and the President. When Air Force capabilities are provided to civil authorities, the relationship is similar to the direct support role of one military force in support of another. Air Force commanders' priorities should be consistent with DOD guidance in these areas. The same is true when Air National Guard (ANG) forces are federalized under Title 10, United States Code (U.S.C.); if in Title 32, U.S.C. or state active duty status, they are under the authority of the state's Adjutant General (TAG), responsible to the state governor (for additional information, see Chapter 2).[15]

JOINT AND MULTINATIONAL ENVIRONMENT

The majority of recent military actions within the homeland have been executed by a joint or combined command structure. Traditional Air Force homeland operations, even if still executed by a commander, Air Force forces (COMAFFOR), are normally executed within a joint organizational structure. Understanding partner roles and missions, as well as supported command direction, is paramount for successful actions.

---

[15] In the case of Washington, D.C., where there is no governor, The Adjutant General reports to the Commanding General of the District of Columbia, who reports to the Secretary of the Army.

Geographic combatant commanders (GCCs) support HD through a layered defense construct (in the forward areas, the approaches, and the homeland itself). US Northern Command (USNORTHCOM), US Pacific Command (USPACOM), and the North American Aerospace Defense Command (NORAD) provide HD in the US, and USNORTHCOM and USPACOM also accomplish DSCA. The GCCs typically serve as the joint force commander (JFC) for their respective areas of responsibility (AORs).

The NORAD treaty established the alliance to conduct airspace warning, airspace control, and maritime warning for a defined portion of North America. USNORTHCOM's AOR also encompasses a defined portion of North America with a broad spectrum of missions assigned in the Unified Command Plan (UCP). Deconflicting the NORAD, USNORTHCOM, and USPACOM missions within the overlapping geographic area is accomplished by SecDef orders and the UCP.

The multitude of commands operating within the US drives the need to deconflict roles, responsibilities, and missions. Successful actions have typically been a result of early planning engagements, understanding and accommodating others' concerns, wide socialization of organizational structures and procedures, as well as continual information flow both vertically and horizontally.

FEDERAL AND STATE AUTHORITIES AND AIR FORCE INVOLVEMENT

Within the homeland, Air Force forces may operate in different statuses. Regardless of the status the forces are in, there should be clarity of the chain of command to support unity of effort. See Chapter 2 for a further discussion of Titles 5, 10 and 32, U.S.C., the impact on the status of Air Force forces operating in the homeland, and the circumstances of dual status command.

There are specific federal laws affecting Air Force personnel and operations in the homeland. The Posse Comitatus Act and the Insurrection Act place limitations on Air Force forces; all Air Force personnel, regardless of status, should be aware of this information.[16]

Posse Comitatus Act (PCA), 18 U.S.C § 1385. The PCA applies within the homeland and by DOD policy also applies to the Departments of the Air Force and Navy, including the U.S. Marine Corps. For homeland operations within the US, this federal statute and the court cases that interpret it place limits on the use of military personnel for civilian law enforcement duties, except as expressly authorized by the Constitution or act of Congress. Specifically prohibited activities include: search and seizure; arrest, apprehension, "stop-and-frisk" detentions and similar activities; and use of military personnel for surveillance or pursuit of individuals, or as undercover agents, informants, investigators, or interrogators. DOD Instruction (DODI) 3025.21, *Defense*

---

[16] For a review of other federal laws affecting homeland operations, see Appendix A.

Support of Civilian Law Enforcement Agencies, identifies several forms of assistance to civilian authorities, which are allowed under the PCA. Exceptions to the PCA include, but are not limited to:

- ☼ Support to law enforcement agencies under 10 U.S.C., Chapter 18.

- ☼ Presidential directed support under the Insurrection Act (see below).

- ☼ Emergency situations involving WMD (10 U.S.C. § 382).

- ☼ Prohibited transactions involving nuclear materials (18 U.S.C. § 831).

- ☼ Counterintelligence support and other missions as approved by the President and the SecDef.

Chapter 18 of 10 U.S.C. §§ 371-382 addresses military support for civilian law enforcement agencies and provides statutory authority for specific types of MSLE. 10 U.S.C. § 375 directs the SecDef to promulgate regulations that prohibit "direct participation by a member of the Army, Navy, Air Force, or Marine Corps in a search, seizure, arrest, or other similar activity unless participation in such activity by such member is otherwise authorized by law."[17]

The Insurrection Act 10 U.S.C. §§ 331-335. These statutory provisions allow the President, at the request of a state governor or legislature, or unilaterally in some circumstances, to employ the armed forces to suppress insurrection against state authority, to enforce federal laws, or to suppress rebellion.

America's constitutional foundations of federalism and limited government place significant trust and responsibility in the capabilities of state and local governments to help protect the American people. State, local, and tribal governments, which best understand their communities and the unique requirements of their citizens, provide first response to incidents through law enforcement, fire, public health, and emergency medical services. They will always play a prominent, frontline role in helping prevent terrorist attacks as well as in preparing for and responding to a range of natural and manmade emergencies.[18]

RANGE OF MILITARY OPERATIONS

The US employs its military capabilities at home and abroad in support of its national security goals in a variety of operations. These operations vary in size, purpose, and combat intensity within a range of military operations (ROMO) that extends from military engagement, security cooperation, and deterrence activities to crisis response and limited contingency operations, and if necessary, major operations

---

[17] This law is expounded upon in DODD 5525.5, *DOD Cooperation with Civilian Law Enforcement Officials* and *AFI 10-801, Assistance to Civilian Law Enforcement Agencies.*
[18] NSHS, 2007.

and campaigns. Most operations within the homeland are at the lower end of the spectrum.

Within the homeland, the concept of the ROMO takes on expanded dimension with respect to authorities and command direction. Civil security and emergency response forces can gain access to a stratum of DOD resources and training through requests supported by the Economy or Stafford Acts.[19] State National Guard forces using either state funded or federal funded equipment can respond at the direction of the state's governor or these forces may be federalized (come under authority of the President with funding from the federal level) and with other regular and reserve forces to accomplish DSCA.

---

[19] See Appendix A.

CHAPTER TWO

COMMAND AND ORGANIZATION

> *Effective unified command is indispensable to response activities and requires a clear understanding of the roles and responsibilities of each participating organization.*
>
> **—National Response Framework, January 2008**

National Response Framework

January 2008

Homeland Security

COMMAND

An understanding of the basic military principles of unity of command and unity of effort is necessary to understand operational command relations within the Homeland.

Unity of command ensures concentration of effort for every objective under one responsible commander. This principle emphasizes that all efforts should be directed and coordinated toward a common objective.[20] **Unity of effort** is critical during interagency operations and can best be achieved through consensus building. The main effort in interagency planning should be to develop a shared, detailed understanding of the situation. This allows the various agencies to better understand how they can best apply their respective capabilities and measure success.[21]

The missions of homeland operations are normally accomplished either within a "whole of government" environment through an interagency process, or through a military structure. The complexity and basic premise of the interagency process for homeland operations, as well as the potential for a surprise terrorist event on American soil, differentiate operations in the homeland from traditional Air Force missions overseas. These differences affect how we organize and present forces.

---

[20] AFDD 1, *Air Force Basic Doctrine, Organization, and Command*, 14 Oct 2011.
[21] Ibid.

An air expeditionary task force (AETF), or equivalent structure in the States, provides the most efficient organizational basis for the Air Force to conduct operations in the homeland, including a command element with A-staff functions, an appropriately tailored air operations center (AOC), and a clearly identified commander. By having a pre-identified or standing command element, key relationships can be established with interagency participants prior to an event. In addition, the staff can be educated and trained on the interagency processes, the NRF, and other areas that add to the complexity of homeland operations. The AETF provides an Air Force command and control (C2) structure to a combatant command, NORAD, or an incident commander under the NRF to achieve operational unity of command and unity of effort when employed in DSCA. Also, each state has a Joint Force Headquarters-State (JFHQ-State) to ensure unity of command and effort for ANG forces, and to provide the interface with the AETF. If agreed upon by the President and the Governor of the state, it may be advantageous to have the commander of the AETF in dual-status, acting in authority over all Air Force forces.

A standing command element, combined with forces capable of response, decreases response time. Asymmetric terrorist attacks often come with minimal or no warning. This stands in contrast to the build-up time typically available before initiation of traditional combat operations. Numerous natural disasters, the response to which may include an Air Force element, may also occur without warning. As a result, homeland operations often require immediate or near-immediate response. To help address the lack of warning, some ANG forces are on a standby basis day-to-day under their governor's authority.

Quick Response through Standing Command Elements

When the alert fighters scrambled during the response to 9/11, the fact they were on alert and tied to a 24/7 chain of command allowed their response to be nearly instantaneous.

This rapid response was again demonstrated by AFNORTH through their staff and standing AOC in 2005 during the preparations for and the aftermath of Hurricanes Katrina and Rita.

Similarly, alert air forces assigned to the Alaskan NORAD Region are on 24/7 tasking from the combined AOC-Alaska to protect critical oil resources and the national missile defense sites in the remote Alaskan homeland.

These standing organizations provide the operational C2 capability necessary for homeland operations in the continental US (CONUS), Alaska, and Asia-Pacific territories.

Operational Control and Administrative Control

Authorities and responsibilities for the two branches of command (operational and administrative) within the homeland are the same as those in any AOR. Additionally, the ANG may conduct state-level homeland operations under the executive authority of a Governor, with commensurate state authorities.

Delegation of operational control (OPCON) over assigned and attached federal military forces conducting homeland operations is accomplished through the commander of USNORTHCOM or USPACOM; and, for specified missions, the NORAD commander. With five combatant commands, NORAD, the Department of the Air Force, and each state's ANG all operating within the homeland, it is important to understand the command relationships when forces are conducting homeland operations.[22] Unity of command of Air Force forces in homeland operations, whether in Title 10, Title 32, or State Active Duty (SAD), is maintained through presentation of forces to the appropriate JFC at the combatant command, subordinate JTF, NORAD, incident command system, or state level.

When personnel are attached to an Air Force Service component for homeland operations, specific administrative control (ADCON) authorities to be exercised by the gaining commander should be specified in appropriate orders. The ADCON requirements associated with Air Reserve Component forces are complex and require legal consideration.

Command of Air Force Formations in Different Legal Statuses

Airmen accomplish HD and provide support to civil authorities under multiple laws and authorities. The Air Force consists of the regular Air Force, the Air National Guard of the United States, the ANG while in the service of the US,[23] and the Air Force Reserve. The authorities are derived from law and statutes which may enable or restrict Airmen's actions.

The status of Airmen is commonly referred to by the legal authority under which they are authorized to perform their assigned missions. These statuses are commonly grouped as:

○ **Title 10, U.S.C.** The regular Air Force, Air Force Reserve, and Air National Guardsmen in federal active duty status are referred to as operating in Title 10 status. Forces are under the authority of the President as commander in chief.[24]

---

[22] A detailed description of these commands can be found later in this chapter.

[23] "ANG means that part of the organized militia of the several States and Territories, Puerto Rico, and the District of Columbia, active and inactive, that—(A) is an air force; (B) is trained, and has its officers appointed, under the sixteenth clause of section 8, article I of the Constitution; (C) is organized, armed, and equipped wholly or partly at Federal expense; and (D) is federally recognized. Air National Guard of the United States means the reserve component of the Air Force all of whose members are members of the ANG." (32 U.S.C. § 101)

[24] 10 U.S.C.

○ **Title 5, U.S.C.** Federal civilian employees, including air reserve technicians (ARTs) in civilian status, fall under Title 5. ARTs are full-time DOD civilian employees, required to serve as members of the Air Force Reserve. They serve under the authority of Title 5 when in civilian status, and under Title 10 when serving as a reservist.

○ **Title 32, U.S.C.** Air National Guardsmen may also be requested to accomplish federal activities, both DSCA and HD, while remaining under the control of the governor. The National Guard also employs civilian technician employees who are uniformed members of the National Guard in a Federal civilian capacity. This is referred to as Title 32 status. They are under the authority of the state governor, but funding is from the federal government.[25]

○ **State Active Duty.** For Air National Guardsmen, when the governor of a state mobilizes the National Guard, the forces are typically in SAD status. They remain under the authority of the governor, exercised through the state's adjutant general, and are funded by the state. SAD forces conduct all state missions in accordance with the needs of the state and within the guidelines of state laws and statutes.

In short, ANG assets can be classified into three categories within the law. With the exception of dual status command under 32 U.S.C. §§ 315 and 325 (see below) requiring approval of the President, they can only be in one status at a time. If agreed beforehand, the joint definition of "coordinating authority" can be used to define the command relationship between commanders in different legal statuses, and allow the state governor to have ANG forces respond to the direction of a Title 10 commander.[26] The Guard forces are still under the authority of the governor, but coordination between the ANG commander and Title 10 commander (i.e., regular officer) is required to achieve unity of effort

Special considerations exist in determining command relationships when dealing with the ANG. **The COMAFFOR exercises OPCON of applicable ANG units and members when they are federalized and in Title 10, U.S.C., status for homeland operations.** ADCON for discipline, personnel support, and administration for these federalized units or members of the ANG is maintained by the 201st Mission Support Squadron at the ANG Readiness Center. However, if full mobilization has occurred, ADCON is transferred to the gaining command. When ANG personnel are involved in training for federal missions (Title 32 status), the commander of the providing command may exercise training and readiness oversight, but not command. Command remains with the state authorities. Guard members in Title 32 status fall under the authority of The Adjutant General (TAG) of their state and therefore their governor. If Guard members operate in Title 32 status outside of their state but within the US, authority will remain with the TAG but be subject to any coordinating authority or state-to-state agreements such as an emergency management assistance compact (EMAC). If no

---

[25] 32 U.S.C. Chapter 1.

[26] For a discussion on coordinating authority, see JP 1, *Doctrine for the Armed Forces of the United States.*

pre-negotiated agreement exists, responsibilities should be coordinated between applicable commanders.

Dual Status Commanders

The following information describes circumstances where commanders in either Title 10 or 32, U.S.C., status can be placed in command of forces from both.

National Guard Dual Status Commander.[27] A unique C2 relationship may be established when Title 10 U.S.C. and National Guard (NG) forces in Title 32, U.S.C., status operate together. Title 32 U.S.C. § 325, allows a single commander to fulfill National Guard (NG) requirements of a NG unit to exercise authority over NG and regular forces while serving on active duty if in command of a NG unit. The President must authorize such service in both duty statuses and the governor of the NG state or territory (or the Commanding General of the District of Columbia NG), consents to such service in both duty statuses. A NG dual status commander retains his state NG commission when ordered to active duty under Title 10 U.S.C. As such, the dual status commander is authorized to command both Title 32 NG and Title 10 federal forces via separate state and federal chains of command. However, if a NG officer is activated to command an active component unit only, then NG requirements cannot be fulfilled by this section of Title 32, U.S.C.

Title 10 Dual Status Commander. 32 U.S.C. § 315 authorizes a Title 10, U.S.C., officer to be detailed by the Secretary of the Air Force (SECAF) to a state NG unit. Such an officer may be tendered a commission in the NG. With the permission of the President, the officer may accept the NG commission without prejudicing his rank and without vacating his regular commission. Once in this dual status, the officer may be appointed to command both state NG and Title 10, U.S.C., forces via separate state and federal chains of command.

A memorandum of agreement (MOA) must be signed by the governor and the President or their respective designees before a dual status command can be established. The MOA should be prepared by staff judge advocates from both chains of command to ensure the concerns of both are addressed. The dual status commander receives orders from a federal chain of command and a state chain of command. As such, the dual status commander is an intermediate link in two distinct, separate chains of command flowing from different sovereigns. While the dual status commander may receive orders from two chains of command, that individual has a duty to exercise all authority in a completely mutually exclusive manner, i.e., either in a federal or state capacity, but never in both capacities at the same time. Additionally, the assigned or attached forces are not dual status. Thus, the commander should take care to ensure the missions of the forces are kept separate. This is best accomplished by maintaining

---

[27] 32 U.S.C. §317. The governor of the state normally is the principal civil authority supported by the primary federal agency and its supporting federal entities. The State Adjutant General or a designee should normally be the principal military authority supported by the dual-status commander when acting in State capacity.

separate staffs for the Title 32 and Title 10 forces, especially separate staff A-2s, A-3s, and legal advisors, so that the separate chains of command remain distinct.

The intent of dual status command is coordination of operations to achieve unity of effort. The NG may be the first military organization engaged at the state level at the incident area. The National Guard Coordination Center (NGCC), in coordination with joint force headquarters (JFHQ) and state joint operation centers (JOC)s, provides situational awareness and status information to the Combatant Commander (CCDR) and other federal stakeholders as the "first line of situational awareness." Likewise, due to the NG's proximity and speed of response, the CCDRs can leverage NG resources and capabilities, including existing C2 structures, into HD operations.

Coordination within Air Force Channels

When considering federal operations, the COMAFFOR should coordinate with the NGB prior to state National Guard involvement. The COMAFFOR may also benefit from placing a liaison at the JFHQ-State and/or the staff of an appointed dual-status commander. Once forces are attached to the COMAFFOR, the COMAFFOR is able to communicate directly with the attached forces. GCC force protection policies take precedence over all force protection policies for programs of any other DOD component deployed in that command's AOR.[28] The defense coordination officer (DCO) is the SecDef point of contact for DOD response. Typically, an AF Emergency Preparedness Liaison Officer (EPLO) is deployed with the defense coordination officer (DCO) to represent the service to the DCO and assist in recommending AF capabilities to support the LFA. For most major DSCA events, an EPLO within the state deploys to the State emergency operations center (EOC) or JFHQ-State during an event and can provide situational awareness to the COMAFFOR.

ORGANIZATION

Unlike other GCCs, there are Air Force forces permanently located within the boundaries of the USNORTHCOM AOR that are not assigned or attached to that combatant command.

Joint and Multinational C2 Elements

While all CCDRs have a role in HD, USNORTHCOM and USPACOM share the primary role in direct defense of the homeland. USNORTHCOM's mission is to conduct HD and DSCA within its assigned AOR of the continental US (CONUS), Alaska, Canada, Mexico, and parts of the Caribbean.[29] USNORTHCOM has Air Forces Northern (AFNORTH) as its Air Force component. USNORTHCOM and AFNORTH are assisted by NORAD, which is a bi-national command (US and Canada) that conducts aerospace warning, control, and maritime warning in defense of North America. The NORAD focus is on three regions: Continental NORAD Region (CONR), Alaskan

---

[28] JP1.

[29] *Unified Command Plan* (2011).

NORAD Region (ANR), and Canadian NORAD Region (CANR). To achieve unity of effort, USNORTHCOM has designated the First Air Force commander as commander and COMAFFOR for both AFNORTH and CONR.

USPACOM's AOR includes Hawaii, the US territories of Guam and American Samoa, and several smaller territories such as Micronesia, the Marshall Islands, and Palau. Pacific Air Forces (PACAF) serves as USPACOM's Air Force component. The Air Force component in Alaska, PACAF's 11 AF, serves multiple roles. USPACOM has established the subunified Alaskan Command, with 11 AF as the air component. The 11 AF commander serves as both commander of Alaskan Command and its COMAFFOR. Under USNORTHCOM, the 11 AF commander serves as both the commander and COMAFFOR of JTF-Alaska (JTF-AK), and commander of NORAD's ANR.

Aligning joint and combined commands and responsibilities with identified Service components achieves unity of effort if not unity of command. When several senior level commands are operating within the same geospatial areas, arranging to have one Service component support all the different higher headquarters achieves unity of effort. Resourcing the Service component and enabling subordinate commands assists in maintaining unity of effort.

Service Force Provider Responsibility for Organizing the Force

With the exception of these C2 nodes, few standing organizations are in place to accomplish homeland operations. Since many homeland operations are in response to emergency or crisis-driven events, organizations should be pre-established to cover response activities.[30] Advance documentation to activate the organization and attach forces can speed the overall deployment process. Force providing organizations should ensure responding forces are provided with the appropriate level of administrative support.

The COMAFFOR, in conjunction with the JFC, may create organizational templates during the deliberate planning process. They can be built within the joint adaptive planning and execution system, deliberate and crisis action planning and execution segments, concept plans or standing operation orders as a starting point to establish organizational structures that can ease the transition to contingency operations. These documents can be refined in crisis action planning (for example, if threatening weather is developing, or there is an increased terrorist threat).

Air Expeditionary Task Force and Subordinate Organizations

A theater COMAFFOR, such as the AFNORTH commander, should be prepared to transfer Air Force forces to a JTF upon direction. In such cases, the COMAFFOR should establish an AETF attached to the JTF as in any other AOR. For example, when Air Force forces are employed in support of USNORTHCOM, they should be presented in the form of an AETF.

---

[30] For specific guidance, see AFI 38-101, *Air Force Organization,* 16 March 2011.

Regardless of the organizational model used, Airmen tend to be spread out during homeland operations, both geographically and organizationally. It is critical that Air Force leadership at all levels maintain accountability of—and full support to—their Airmen.

Integrating with National Guard Operating in Support of Civil Authorities

During an operation, the COMAFFOR should be aware that the initial response will likely be from the state National Guard. Subsequently, Air Force (ANG) capabilities may be requested through an emergency management assistance compact (EMAC) request to other states at the state governmental level. Should the event be of sufficient scale, federal capabilities may be requested in accordance with the NRF. See Chapter 4 for greater detail.

FORCE PRESENTATION FOR DSCA

DSCA may be provided to civil organizations through a variety of methods. The vehicle by which the request is made will shape how the DOD response occurs. For instance, the National Oceanic and Atmospheric Administration receives support from an Air Force weather reconnaissance squadron (the "Hurricane Hunters") by congressional stipulation in the annual DOD appropriation process. Alternatively, the National Interagency Fire Center receives the support of C-130s carrying modular airborne firefighting systems through Economy Act agreements. The most visible means of providing DSCA, particularly when natural disasters occur, is when Air Force capabilities are provided to assist through the NRF, as authorized by the Stafford Act.

The overall coordination of federal response activities is implemented through the Secretary of the Department of Homeland Security (DHS) consistent with HSPD 5 and the NRF. Other federal departments and agencies carry out their response authorities and responsibilities within this overarching construct. If DOD involvement is not necessary, the DHS Secretary appoints a primary federal officer as the on-scene coordinator known as the FCO. If DOD involvement is needed, the SecDef directs commander, USNORTHCOM (CDRUSNORTHCOM) or commander, USPACOM (CDRUSPACOM), as appropriate, to assign the DCO as the single voice for DOD. DCOs are assigned to each Federal Emergency Management Agency (FEMA) region and are full time active duty Army officers in the grade of O-6.

The DCO's role may vary depending upon the scale of an event. The DCO, and the Defense Coordinating Element staff, coordinates DOD capabilities between the FCO and DOD. Additionally, for a small event, the DCO may direct USNORTHCOM/USPACOM Service component response efforts.[31] If DOD involvement becomes extensive, then CDRUSNORTHCOM or CDRUSPACOM may establish a JTF or response task force that would receive OPCON of forces. In this case, the DCO becomes the JTF or response task force commander's liaison to the federal agencies.

---

[31] National Contingency Plan 0-2, *Civil Support Concept of Employment*

Air Force Capabilities for DSCA

Most Air Force support to civil authorities will be in already familiar roles—conducting airlift of supplies to affected areas or providing medical or engineering assistance to people in need. Examples of Air Force capabilities that may be requested in a domestic disaster or emergency include (but are not limited to):

✪ **Air mobility.** The Air Force may provide airlift to support local, state, DOD, or other federal agencies (e.g., aeromedical evacuation).

✪ **Airbase opening and sustainment.** The Air Force provides AETF force modules to open an airbase, provide C2, establish an airbase, generate the mission, operate an airbase, and robust the airbase. These modules can be used to establish remote, abandoned, or inactive airfields with capabilities to accomplish an assigned mission; the capabilities can also be used to augment existing airfield facilities to handle the demands of a homeland security incident.

✪ **Communications.** Deployable Air Force communications systems can provide worldwide, single-channel, secure voice and record communications, and secure on-site communications at or away from home stations.

✪ **Reconnaissance.** The Air Force can provide reconnaissance capabilities, both analysis/assessment capabilities and assets (e.g., unmanned aerial vehicles; AF Auxiliary, space reconnaissance assets), to monitor designated locations and provide airborne surveillance. They could, for example, be used to monitor floodwaters, assess hurricane or tornado damage, or assist in tracking terrorist activities. Reconnaissance assets could also be used to collect airborne nuclear debris following a domestic nuclear event. (Note that national intelligence oversight policies [Executive Order (EO) 12333 and others] may limit DOD entities' intelligence roles within the US and similarly restrict the collection and retention of information on US persons.)

✪ **Investigative support.** Air Force Office of Special Investigations (AFOSI) can provide investigative expertise to support criminal investigations and counterintelligence services.

✪ **Search and rescue.** Air Force assets can provide rapid response capability for search, transportation, insertion, and extraction functions in support of rescue activities, as well as initial treatment of medical and other needs..

✪ **Civil engineer support.** Air Force civil engineer forces are capable of rapidly responding to worldwide contingency operations. Capabilities include operation and maintenance of facilities and infrastructure, aircraft rescue and facility fire suppression, construction management of emergency repair activities, supporting the cross-functional EM program integrating preparedness, response, recovery, and mitigation activities, and explosive ordnance disposal (EOD). EOD responds to all incidents involving military munitions and provides assistance to federal, state, and

19

local law enforcement agencies with EOD matters when determined to be in the interest of public safety. EOD supports specialized JTF operations and hazardous materials response for incidents involving explosives.

✪ **Health Services.** Air Force Medical Service capabilities, while primarily designed to meet a wartime mission, are easily adaptable for civil disaster response. Small, incremental packages of tailored medical capability can be rapidly deployed to meet immediate and short-term civilian requirements.

The list above is intended to provide examples of the breadth of capabilities the Air Force can bring to its DSCA role. It is not all-inclusive, but conveys the large variety of responses to DSCA needs the Air Force can perform.

Opportune Support to Law Enforcement Agencies

The PCA restricts direct federal military involvement for federal law enforcement purposes, except as authorized by Congress and the US Constitution (see Appendix A). National Guard forces in a Title 32 status are not subject to the PCA. If Air Force forces are used in a law enforcement role they must be in compliance with public law. Air Force Security Forces and AFOSI may be called on for their expertise and the tactical level employment of these forces should be in accordance with their training. Intelligence components and intelligence component capabilities may also be used to support LEA. Such support requires SECDEF approval unless information is acquired in an incidental manner.[32] Additionally, other support can also be provided (training, expert advice, etc.) per applicable authorities.[33]

COMMAND RELATIONSHIPS

In order to properly plan and execute homeland operations, an understanding of command relationships is required. This section outlines the roles and responsibilities of relevant command elements.

Geographic Combatant Commanders

CDRUSNORTHCOM and CDRUSPACOM are GCCs with responsibilities for conducting homeland operations. USPACOM is unique in that the forces in Alaska are under the combatant command (COCOM) of CDRUSPACOM, but Alaska is in the USNORTHCOM AOR. To facilitate operations in Alaska, CDRUSNORTHCOM has established JTF-Alaska (JTF-AK), staffed by CDRUSPACOM's Alaskan Command. The 11 AF commander, as joint force air component commander (JFACC), employs the 611 AOC to support JTF-AK missions as well as ANR missions. This arrangement allows for retention of unity of command and effort in presenting Air Force forces to CDRUSNORTHCOM. If additional forces are needed for a mission under

---

[32] See DoDD 5240.01-R, DoDD 5525.5, AFI 14-104, *Oversight of Intelligence Activities,* and AFI 14-119, *Intelligence Support to Force Protection.*
[33] DoDD 3025.18, *Defense Support of Civil Authorities*, DoDD 5525.5, and AFI 10-801.

USNORTHCOM control, the SecDef may direct the attachment of forces from another command.

Incidents occurring in the homeland within the USPACOM AOR are normally organized around the JTF construct with forces attached from USPACOM's assigned forces. But, as in any other operation, if USPACOM does not have the resident capability required to handle the situation then the SecDef may attach forces from elsewhere as necessary. USNORTHCOM has very few assigned forces, so in most cases the SecDef will attach forces from another combatant command, or forces which are normally unassigned.

If a domestic incident occurs, CDRUSNORTHCOM or CDRUSPACOM may establish a JTF to provide C2 for the DOD response force. In the NORTHCOM AOR, the air component to the JTF would normally be in the form of an AETF and the AFNORTH commander, or his designee, would be the COMAFFOR. In some situations there may not be a need to attach Air Force forces to the JTF and AFNORTH may assume a direct support role to the JTF. In the USPACOM AOR, the PACAF commander designates the COMAFFOR. In Alaska, where NORTHCOM has responsibility for homeland security but forces are under the COCOM of CDRUSPACOM, PACAF provides the 11 AF commander, as the COMAFFOR supporting the USNORTHCOM JTF-Alaska.

There are instances where the military capability for an incident resides in a single Service and it makes sense to create a task force for only that one Service's forces. If the Air Force is so tasked, it may establish an AETF. In this case, due to the established relationships and role previously described, the AETF commander would not serve as the COMAFFOR but remain subordinate to the current designated COMAFFOR. As in all other task forces, command arrangements are approved by the CCDR. See Air Force Doctrine Document (AFDD) 1.

Functional Combatant Commanders

In the area of HD, US Strategic Command (USSTRATCOM) may expect to be the supported command for DOD space and information operations, especially computer network defense. USSTRATCOM is responsible for warning and, if necessary, assessing missile attack to the other CCDRs. It is tasked as a supporting command to NORAD to provide missile warning and space surveillance in furtherance of NORAD's mission of aerospace control of North America. In addition, USSTRATCOM would support USNORTHCOM and USPACOM in the event military operations are required to protect the homeland. Moreover, United States Cyber Command, a sub-unified command under USSTRATCOM, has as support relationship to HD through DOD's Integrated Cyber Center that supports the DHS National Cyber security and Communications Integration Center.

US Transportation Command (USTRANSCOM) serves as the DOD single manager for transportation, providing common-user air, land, and sea transportation and terminal services to meet national security objectives. These security objectives can occur in the homeland and USTRANSCOM will normally be in a supporting role. Air Mobility Command (AMC) is USTRANSCOM's air component, and the Air Force's manager for air mobility. Its mission is to provide airlift, air refueling, special air missions, and aeromedical evacuation in support of national objectives. These capabilities support humanitarian, HD, DSCA, and other operations. Through 18 AF (Air Forces Transportation [AFTRANS]), AMC provides these capabilities to USTRANSCOM, and in turn, to other commands.

US Special Operations Command (USSOCOM) serves as a supported or supporting commander for designated global strike operations and selected counterterrorism activities. The commander, USSOCOM serves as the supporting commander to CDRUSNORTHCOM and CDRUSPACOM within their respective AORs when requirements exceed conventional forces' capabilities or special operations forces expertise is needed. When directed by the President or the SecDef, CDRUSSOCOM conducts special operations and provides special operations forces as required in support of civil authorities during DSCA operations, with Air Force Special Operations Command providing the Air Force personnel and materiel. USSOCOM may also provide liaison officers and other assistance to the supported CCDRs.

North American Aerospace Defense Command (NORAD)

NORAD has responsibility for providing air sovereignty, air warning, and air defense of the North American continent, specifically the CONUS, Alaska, Canada, Puerto Rico, and the US Virgin Islands. NORAD is a bi-national command, with two chains of command. One chain of command goes to the Canadian Prime Minister and the other to the President. **Air Force air assets supporting NORAD fall under the OPCON of the NORAD commander in his role as commander, US Element NORAD, with OPCON delegated to the respective NORAD regional air defense commanders (i.e., ANR/CC and CONR/CC).** Each region has a commander triple-hatted as JFACC, airspace control authority (ACA), and area air defense commander for executing defensive counterair (DCA) missions. The commanders of ANR and CONR do not have OPCON over entire Air Force units; rather they have OPCON over specific personnel and assets, once attached, conducting the DCA mission. NORAD air defense sectors execute tactical control of DCA assets as designated in the regional air tasking order published by the First Air Force AOC and Combined Air Operations Center Alaska. USSTRATCOM supports NORAD by providing the necessary missile warning and space surveillance.

Other Elements of the Air Component

Below are standing Air Force organizations which aid in homeland operations.

☼ **Air Force National Security Emergency Preparedness Directorate (AFNSEP).** This AFNORTH directorate is responsible for integrating DSCA mission considerations into contingency plans and exercise scenarios. They also coordinate mission requirements with combatant commands and civilian agencies for planning, training, and execution. During DSCA events, they provide trained Emergency Preparedness Liaison Officers (EPLOs) to represent the Air Force to the DCO and civilian agencies. To support USPACOM, AFNSEP deploys EPLOs to Hawaii, Guam, and other U.S. Territories/Commonwealths in the Pacific when required. In these cases, AFNORTH maintains OPCON of the EPLOs, and transfers tactical control to the DCO supporting PACOM.[34]

⚙ **Air Force Auxiliary (AFAux)/Civil Air Patrol (CAP).** The AFAux/CAP is a federally chartered corporation for the purposes of promoting aviation education and fostering local civil aviation. It is authorized, when directed by the SECAF, to fulfill any non-combat mission of the Air Force. When CAP operates in AFAux status, it is an Air Force federal military activity and as such is required to comply with the PCA and intelligence oversight restrictions. Air Education and Training Command supports AFAux/CAP operations. NORTHCOM or PACOM request assistance through AETC ISO DSCA during response and recovery operations, and other federal operations.

The AFAux/CAP provides low-cost platforms using light aircraft that can be used

> AFAux/CAP assets, much like the ANG, can be classified into two categories within the law and can only be in one status at a time. The first category is Title 10, where these Air Force Auxiliary forces are deemed an instrumentality of the United States when carrying out a non-combat mission assigned by the Secretary of the Air Force. The second category is where these same individuals and equipment are acting in the CAP Corporate category under Title 36 as a federally sanctioned non-profit corporation.
>
> **—Information derived from Titles 10 and 36, U.S.C.**

for non-combat missions such as search and rescue (SAR), critical infrastructure protection, low-level route survey or reconnaissance over high-value national infrastructure locations.

⚙ **Air Force Rescue Coordination Center (AFRCC).** CDRUSNORTHCOM delegates mission coordinator responsibilities for day-to-day search and rescue (SAR) to the COMAFFOR (AFNORTH/CC). The COMAFFOR, as JFACC, executes via the AFRCC located within AFNORTH's 601 AOC. The center coordinates all inland SAR response within the CONUS according to the National SAR Plan. Duties include searching for missing/overdue aircraft, managing beacon alerts, and assisting the states with their SAR missions. The AFRCC validates all requests and brokers federal assistance on an "ask, not task" basis to save life and prevent undue suffering. Similarly, the 11th Rescue Coordination Center performs the same mission within Alaska.

---

[34] All Air Force EPLOs are reservists, and therefore Air Force Reserve Command (AFRC) may have ADCON depending on duty status.

In accordance with the National SAR Plan, these functions are performed by the US Coast Guard for the state of Hawaii, and USPACOM for US territories in the Pacific.

Joint Task Forces

When a crisis requires a military response, the geographic CCDR will usually form a tailored JTF. If Air Force forces are attached to the JTF, they stand up as an AETF within the JTF. The AETF commander, designated as the COMAFFOR, provides the single Air Force face to the JTF commander. For example, USNORTHCOM's COMAFFOR, the AFNORTH commander, shares a relationship with state level JTFs when they are stood up and he may use the 601 AOC, or other organic capabilities to his command, to support state level operations, as necessary.

Multiple COMAFFORs may be appointed within the homeland with each one assigned to a task- or event-specific JTF (e.g. JTF-Civil Support, JTF-North and JTF-National Capital Region all operate within the homeland). Coordination among all the JTFs should be taken into account when operations cross their respective geographic areas. The COMAFFOR (theater or JTF) should be cognizant of the multiple other JTFs and JTF-like entities in the interagency environment already existing in the AOR and should establish relationships with them.

OTHER AUTHORITIES

Along with those command authorities already discussed, there are some other authoritative duties the COMAFFOR should consider.

Airspace Control

Airspace control includes coordinating and deconflicting air traffic. Unlike in other AORs where the COMAFFOR is normally delegated airspace control authority by the JFC,[35] in homeland operations this responsibility is almost always retained by the Federal Aviation Administration (FAA). All airspace planning is coordinated with and approved by the FAA. The FAA provides liaisons to USNORTHCOM and USPACOM to collaborate and minimize conflicts during mission execution. In the event the FAA is unable to uphold these responsibilities, the COMAFFOR should be prepared to take over the ACA role.

Incident Awareness and Assessment

Incident awareness and assessment is similar to intelligence, surveillance, and reconnaissance, but conducted within the US for civil support operations.[36] There are restrictions to protect the privacy of US citizens that require thorough legal review

---

[35] JP 3-30, *Command and Control for Joint Air Operations*, 12 January 2010.
[36] AFDD 2-0, *Global Integrated Intelligence, Surveillance & Reconnaissance Operations*, 6 January 2012.

before committing military assets. Their employment need not be prohibited, but usage should be carefully considered. For example, using unmanned aircraft for DSCA requires SecDef approval but may be useful in providing damage assessment or aiding in rescue efforts after a major storm.[37]

A variety of organizations, such as the Federal Bureau of Investigations (FBI), National Counterterrorism Center, DHS, as well as state and local law enforcement can provide much of the information normally required. Coordinating with these agencies is advised before collecting data independently. For more guidance, see AFDD 2-0.

Space Coordinating Authority

Space assets provide considerable capability to homeland operations, such as communications and imaging. Space coordinating authority is a specific authority delegated to a commander for coordinating specific space functions and activities. It is normally delegated from the JFC to the theater COMAFFOR. In order to plan, execute, and assess space operations, the COMAFFOR typically designates a director of space forces to coordinate and integrate space capabilities into an operation. For more information, see AFDD 3-14, *Space Operations*.

---

[37] DODD 3025.18. *Defense Support of Civil Authorities (DSCA)*, 29 December 2010. Approval level and authorities for support to civil agencies will vary depending on purpose of the mission. Commanders, operators, and intelligence personnel should work closely with their legal support staff to ensure this is done correctly.

CHAPTER THREE

PLANNING, EXECUTION, AND ASSESSMENT

Think ahead. Don't let day-to-day operations drive out planning.

— Donald Rumsfeld

Planning, execution, and assessment are critical to success in any endeavor. In relation to homeland operations, all three phases require an understanding of the threat, as well as the roles of various other government agencies. It is also important to understand the Air Force's role is broader than just air operations. The Service can employ a variety of other capabilities to support operations within the homeland.

HOMELAND DEFENSE

The defense of the homeland is not entirely unique, and should primarily follow established war-fighting doctrine. As discussed in Chapter 2, however, the command structure for homeland operations is more complex than in most AORs. NORAD and USNORTHCOM both have responsibilities within the same US air domain. CDRUSNORTHCOM and CDRUSPACOM are GCCs, each with a chain of command through the SecDef to the President. NORAD is a bi-national command, with two chains of command. One chain of command goes to the Canadian Prime Minister and the other to the US President. As a result, C2 relationships should be emphasized in planning to ensure people understand their chain of command, and from whom they take orders during certain events.

Alaska in particular is an environment that requires C2 clarity. Air Force forces there are assigned to USPACOM, while the defense of Alaska is a USNORTHCOM responsibility. Clarity of command is provided through JTF-AK and Alaskan Command. Similarly, while Hawaii, Guam, and other US territories in the Pacific are a part of the homeland, CDRUSPACOM is the GCC responsible for those locations.

The airpower tenet of "centralized control, decentralized execution" remains relevant in homeland operations. **Due to a variety of legal and political factors,**

homeland operations will very likely lean in the direction of "centralized execution" more so than in operations outside the homeland. Senior decision makers continually balance the need for aggressive and effective operations with the need to minimize collateral damage and casualties. They most effectively accomplish this through applying risk management controls and processes.

When execution is more centralized, the ability to engage fleeting targets decreases. One compensatory measure is to have well established and understood rules of engagement (ROE) and rules for the use of force (RUF). To be effective, the ROE/RUF should be clearly understood and rapidly executable. For example, in a counterair role the shooter must receive approval in time to destroy the target. ROE/RUF should be clearly defined for the full spectrum of potential response actions.

DEFENSE SUPPORT OF CIVIL AUTHORITIES

Many of the capabilities inherent in air forces can also provide for rapid response to support civil authorities in cases of domestic emergencies and disasters. **Air Force forces support federal, state, and local civil authorities in cases of natural or man-made domestic emergencies, civil disturbances, or authorized law enforcement activities under the concepts of DSCA.** Planning for and responding to these events should be a Total Force effort.

Acts of terrorism, natural disasters, and accidents involving hazardous materials stretch local and state emergency response resources to the limit, and sometimes beyond. For acts or threats of terrorism in the US, the DOJ, acting through the FBI, is the lead agency. When disasters or accidents occur, local authorities lead the effort and request assistance from state (e.g., "non-federalized" National Guard) or federal agencies as needed. In both instances, regular and reserve military units, including Air Force civilian personnel, may be tasked to assist in response and recovery efforts. In all cases, the Air Force is prepared to support homeland operations through intelligence and information sharing.

Installation commanders plan for situations that would require assigned units to assist local authorities. They and their staffs should be aware of the various industries or other facilities in the surrounding community, and should assess what potential hazard or threat these industries and facilities may pose to the installation. They should also determine what type of assistance each may require in the event of an emergency. The operational risk management process should be integral to any planning related to homeland operations. Installation commanders should also be aware of critical dependencies on the surrounding community and work with involved agencies to ensure the installation is capable of continuing minimum essential functions in an emergency. **Coordinated planning between the installation and the community is critical to a successful emergency response and should take into account the need to preserve the installation's ability to project and protect its forces when and where needed.** What occurs in the community may affect the installation's ability to perform its mission. In addition to providing support, Air Force installations should have plans and procedures in place for receiving aid and assistance from DOD or civil agencies when needed.

Memoranda of agreement or understanding (MOA/MOU) with the surrounding communities can clarify such issues as response procedures and capabilities, and reimbursement of costs. MOA and MOU provide a means to answer numerous questions before a disaster or accident occurs, and allow for planning as to how military units will respond and what the local authorities expect of them. Governors may also have EMACs.

Key agencies for planning include local fire, medical, and police forces. During off-base emergency situations, the Air Force may be able to provide assistance fighting fires, treating the injured, or evacuating buildings.

The NRF contains detailed guidance and planning considerations, and it should be the primary reference in developing MOA/MOU. Refer to the NRF and take the following into consideration when drafting an MOA/MOU:

- ✪ **Installation commanders may provide immediate response to save lives, prevent human suffering, or mitigate great property damage resulting from any civil emergency or attack.**[38]. Immediate response authority only applies when local capability is overwhelmed, triggered by a request from civil authorities, under imminently serious conditions, and with no time to see approval from higher authority. The requirement to employ assets under Immediate Response Authority should be reassessed at least every 72 hours. Otherwise, SecDef approval is required prior to providing Air Force support. Commanders acting under immediate response authority will expeditiously notify the JDOMS through command channels.

- ✪ Determine the circumstances under which mutual response will be requested and provided between the parties named in the memorandum. The circumstances vary from installation to installation depending on available capabilities for both the off-base and on-base organizations, as well as what types of industries are located in the off-base communities. Common examples of requested assistance are firefighting, explosive ordnance disposal (EOD), or hazardous materials handling.

- ✪ There should be a written set of instructions that civil authorities can follow when requesting assistance. This will standardize request procedures and clarify requirements for both the military and civilian organizations involved.

- ✪ Legal authority for DOD participation vary by the severity of the incident, e.g., declaration of a major disaster, or request under the Economy Act, or mutual aid request permitted by a specific regulation. These triggers are important, ensuring

---

[38] DODD 3025.18.

all parties understand when the MOA will apply and ensuring proper expenditure of DOD funds.

⊙ Specific procedures should be provided for use by responding units when reporting to the scene of an emergency. Specify how the military organization will integrate with the civil authorities. A section within a MOA should also include frequencies for radios, radio procedures, equipment requirements, personnel requirements, force protection requirements, etc.

⊙ A section within a MOA should contain instructions on how to track costs and request reimbursement. It applies to both the military and civilian agencies since most MOA/MOU are mutual response agreements.

⊙ A MOA/MOU should specify such things as minimum notification time before assistance is withdrawn, maximum amount of time assistance can be provided, and procedures for transferring responsibilities to relieving units.

⊙ Procedures for conducting joint exercises to familiarize all parties with the command structure and the scenarios in which assistance might be rendered should be incorporated into a MOA/MOU.[39]

⊙ A section in a MOA/MOU should describe efforts to bring all DOD installations clustered in one greater community together into an integrated, community-wide support plan.

PLANNING AND ASSESSMENT

AFFOR staffs and air operations centers (AOC) provide the full spectrum of planning and assessment in support of homeland operations. A specific AOC provides support for each homeland AOR, aligned by both geographic combatant command and NORAD region. Geographically, USNORTHCOM is supported by AFNORTH's 601 AOC, with the exception of Alaska. Alaskan operations are run by USNORTHCOM's Joint Task Force-Alaska (JTF-AK), supported by the 611 AOC. USPACOM is supported by PACAF's 613 AOC for the Pacific region. Similarly, CONR is supported by the 601 AOC, and the ANR is supported by the 611 AOC.[40]

Additionally, each of these AOCs is in turn supported by USTRANSCOM for air refueling, airlift, aeromedical evacuation, and specialized airlift missions. This support is provided by USTRANSCOM's air component (AFTRANS) via the 618 AOC (Tanker Airlift Control Center).

---

[39] See AFI 10-2501 for emergency management, off-base exercise, and coordination requirements with local communities.

[40] NORAD assists the defense of Canada via CANR, supported by Canada's CANR AOC. The territories protected by PACAF's 613 AOC, such as Hawaii and Guam, do not fall within the auspices of NORAD and therefore do not have a parallel NORAD mission.

Assessment procedures in accordance with Joint Publication 5-0 should be utilized to determine the effectiveness and performance of mission execution in support of homeland operations.

PREPAREDNESS AND RESPONSE

Many events, from terrorist attacks to natural disasters, often occur with little or no warning. Terrorists attempt to hit quickly and decisively. A natural disaster, such as a hurricane, can begin as an event believed to be controllable, but can rapidly spiral upward into one requiring greatly increased response needs. One of the best ways to mitigate those realities is to lean forward within the existing legal and policy framework. There are a number of options available for the Air Force to be fully prepared.

Installation commanders should possess a comprehensive and effective emergency management program. Preparation of standing orders provides for better readiness and faster response by the Air Force. These can include prepare to deploy orders, establish direct liaison authorized (DIRLAUTH) relationships, command relationships, and other responsibilities, all before an incident occurs. They can also include force modules with unit type codes identified, sourced, and alerted to be ready for deployment within a certain notification window. DIRLAUTH allows subordinate echelons to establish relationships within the interagency community, cross-flow information, and refine plans and potential support requests. Similarly, concepts of operations help the air component prepare to act by documenting various processes, policies, and plans well before the event takes place. Headquarters, Air Combat Command is the lead agent for the Air Force's homeland security concepts of operations. Lastly, the standing C2 elements previously discussed enable the air component to lean forward. Once identified, the COMAFFOR and staff can become experts on the plans and policies affecting operations in the homeland, ones that are substantially different than those impacting traditional operations.

In anticipation of being tasked during an actual emergency, commanders can recall personnel, run mobility processes, palletize equipment, and accomplish any other preparatory actions that will minimize the response timeline. **Existing rules prohibit actual deployment of personnel until a formal request has been made, unless an immediate response resulting from a civil emergency or attack is required to save lives, prevent human suffering, or mitigate great property damage.**

IMMEDIATE RESPONSE

Imminently serious conditions resulting from any civil emergency or attack may require immediate action by military commanders or by responsible officials of other DOD agencies to save lives, prevent human suffering, or mitigate great property damage. **When such conditions exist and time does not permit prior approval from higher headquarters, local military commanders and responsible officials of other DOD components are authorized to take necessary action to respond to requests of civil authorities, with follow-on reporting up the appropriate**

command chain as soon as practicable. Immediate Response Authority only applies when local capability is overwhelmed and is triggered by a request from civil authorities under imminently serious conditions with no time to seek approval from higher authority. The requirement to employ assets under Immediate Response Authority should be reassessed at least every 72 hours.

INITIAL RESPONSE

The formal request for assistance process takes time. From the moment the initial request is sent to the DOD until military forces are on scene, critical time elapses that may result in extensive human suffering and property damage. There are actions the component commanders can take in the interim. The commanders of AFNORTH and PACAF are dual-hatted as component commanders and the Air Force regional planning agents for DSCA in their respective CCDRs' AORs. The respective AFNORTH and PACAF staff expertise and designated operations centers play a central role in providing component-level initial support to civil authorities.

In general, to execute a component-level initial response effort, the regional planning agents should:

✪ Quickly establish lines of communication to facilitate requests for assistance, as well as coordinate with the respective CCDR and civil authorities.

✪ Develop COAs appropriate for Air Force support and response capabilities.

✪ Perform operational risk management categorizing hazards and assigning risk controls to the appropriate level of leadership.

✪ Source Air Force assets.

✪ Establish lines of command and control for Air Force forces.

✪ Plan for the efficient hand-off to follow-on forces.

INCIDENT MANAGEMENT ACTIONS

When the SecDef approves use of military forces to aid in a domestic incident, the corresponding combatant command will establish a command structure to conduct the response, incorporating the appropriate Air Force response forces and capabilities. Air Force organizations use the AFIMS structure to organize response forces for compatibility and integration with domestic response organization incident management systems. As the operation progresses, military forces will receive direction from civil authorities on how to respond; this will continue until the emergency subsides. Air Force forces should be used for what they have been trained for: civil engineer personnel can be used to help provide incident C2 in accordance with the National Incident

Management System (NIMS). Medical professionals can treat the sick and wounded. Airlift forces can be used to transport humanitarian supplies.

SUPPORT TO CIVILIAN LAW ENFORCEMENT

The PCA restricts direct military involvement for law enforcement purposes, except as authorized by Congress and the US Constitution (see Appendix A), called military support to civilian law enforcement agencies. **If Air Force forces are used in a law enforcement role they must be in compliance with public law.** Normally Air Force force protection assets, such as Security Forces and AFOSI, will be called on for their expertise and the tactical level employment of these forces should be in accordance with their training.

In addition, law enforcement agencies may frequently request a variety of reconnaissance capabilities. Reconnaissance is an area in which the DOD has a tremendous capability edge over civilian agencies. The use of military reconnaissance assets is not expressly prohibited, however there are numerous legal implications associated with reconnaissance activities that require thorough legal reviews in advance of conducting such operations.

NATIONAL SPECIAL SECURITY EVENTS

Terrorist attacks against highly visible, well-attended events can have a significant impact on our country because of the physical and psychological damage. When designated by the Secretary of Homeland Security, in accordance with 18 U.S.C. § 3056, these events are called national special security events (NSSE). Examples include the State of the Union Address and national political party conventions. Presidential Decision Directive 62, *Protection Against Unconventional Threats to the Homeland and Americans Overseas* reaffirms the domestic lead agencies and their responsibilities. It outlines the roles and responsibilities of other federal agencies, including the Public Health Service, the Environmental Protection Agency, the Department of Energy, the FBI, the US Secret Service, FEMA, and others. **Air Force forces can provide a wide range of support, such as assisting in C2, air patrols, medical support, military working dogs, logistical support, and response if a crisis occurs. Many of the NSSE are vulnerable to air threats, so an air sovereignty mission is expected.**

DEFENSE OF CRITICAL INFRASTRUCTURE ASSETS

Certain infrastructure within the US is critical to the defense and normal function of the nation. If this infrastructure were disrupted by a man-made or natural disaster, it could cause grave damage. Examples include national missile defense sites, the National Capital Region, and electrical generation plants. DOD can be called on to help protect such installations from attack and to respond if a disaster occurs. An analysis of the nation's vulnerabilities in this area is extremely sensitive and highly classified. The

Air Force should be prepared in case it is called on to detect, preempt, respond to, mitigate, and recover from any potential threat to the nation's critical infrastructure.

MILITARY ASSISTANCE TO CIVIL DISTURBANCES

The Insurrection Act is an exception to the normal prohibition of military forces performing direct law enforcement duties in the civilian communities. Under certain conditions the President may invoke this act to send in DOD forces to help control a situation.[41] If Air Force forces are employed, they should normally be trained and equipped to handle civil disturbances and operate under very specific ROE/RUF. Since National Guard forces in state status and under the control of a governor do not have the same restrictions (for PCA purposes) as active duty forces, they may be the force of choice.

INTERAGENCY COOPERATION

When a domestic incident occurs, many federal, state, and local agencies will be involved. Air Force personnel should be aware of the different agencies to facilitate effective and efficient support. With the exception of HD missions, a civilian agency will be in charge of the incident and military assistance will be similar to a direct support role.

Although the Air Force can provide many capabilities, often there is another Service or agency better suited to a particular mission. For example, the Air Force has the ability to respond with CBRN forces and medical teams. However, depending on the scenario, the Centers for Disease Control may be the more appropriate agency to respond to a biological incident.

The COMAFFOR should have a clear understanding of the capabilities, shortfalls, and legal limitations on the use of his forces. The COMAFFOR and his staff should also have a similar understanding of other agencies in order to plan appropriately. By leveraging the strengths and weaknesses of all agencies, and building strong peace-time relationships, the COMAFFOR can help assure mission success as a whole.

LEAD FEDERAL AGENCIES

During an emergency or other event, there may be a lead federal agency (LFA) designated. A LFA is defined as the federal agency that leads and coordinates the overall federal response to an emergency. Designation and responsibilities of a lead federal agency vary according to the type of emergency and the agency's statutory authority.[42] When planning Air Force responses to potential scenarios, Airmen should

---

[41] See DoD 5300.27, *The Code of Federal regulations of the United States of America*, and DoDD 3025.12.
[42] JP 3-41, *Chemical, Biological, Radiological, and Nuclear Consequence Management*, 21 June 2012.

consider which agency could be designated as the LFA. Planners should discern the legal charge and authorities of LFAs to better understand how the COMAFFOR can seamlessly employ Airmen to assist during an incident.

CHAPTER FOUR

EMERGENCY PREPAREDNESS

> *The policy of the United States is to have sufficient capabilities at all levels of government to meet essential defense and civilian needs during any national security emergency.*
>
> **—Executive Order 12656,** *Assignment of Emergency Preparedness Responsibilities*

A great deal of DOD's planning efforts for homeland operations focus on DSCA, and more specifically, EP. Any Air Force capability, including intelligence capabilities, may be used in the DSCA context provided there is adherence to applicable federal law and there is no interference with military readiness or operations. Air Force leaders charged with an EP mission should anticipate what capabilities they could provide during an emergency, and how best to prepare.

LOCAL PREPARATIONS

At the local level, first responders will include fire, police, and medical personnel. They will initiate the incident command system in accordance with their local procedures. If the situation escalates and requires state or federal support on scene, the respective local, state, and federal chains of command remain separate. Local efforts remain under the control of their local leadership. State efforts are under the control of the governor and federal efforts ultimately fall under the control of the President but they will all work together within the unified management system creating joint action plan as directed by the NIMS and the NRF.

Normal day-to-day preparation activities include the creation of MOU/MOAs between military installation commanders and local municipal leaders for capability support as discussed in Chapter 3. Military and civilian units should test the functionality of these agreements through local response exercises. Personnel should also meet regularly to discuss relevant issues, such as training, manning, and funding. This also serves as a way to maintain relationships between the base and local community. Such partnerships can significantly reduce friction and increase effectiveness during an actual disaster response.

At the installation level, upgraded EP planning and training is coupled with other efforts; including counterterrorism, antiterrorism, critical infrastructure protection, mission assurance, and information assurance for Air Force infrastructure and personnel to both instill solid passive defense measures and allow a coordinated approach to installation and community protection. Combining these protection measures with the Air Force incident management system and continuity of operations planning will give local base offices the tools to maintain or seize the initiative after attack. For the longer term, networks of DOD installations will be integrated into the local community's preparation and response scheme with rapid detection, response, and incident management capabilities.

Local base commanders may have their installation identified as a support location. There are three major designations that Air Force commanders may be called upon to support.

- ○ **Incident Support Base.** An extension of the National Distribution System which includes distribution centers as well as sites positioned to enable a resource management and provisioning capability. This is vital to ensure that resources are in or near the area of disaster impact for immediate distribution upon direction of the appropriate state and federal officials. These resources remain national assets until directed forward to points of distribution where the state takes control. When a DOD installation is selected as an incident support base, its purpose is to support the LFA and the supporting personnel and equipment.

- ○ **Federal Team Staging Facility (FTSF).** An installation or facility designated by the LFA and used by supporting agency to mass responding forces for employment when the full responsibilities of an incident support base are not required.

- ○ **The Base Support Installation (BSI).** Normally a DOD installation with an airfield and suitable support facilities.[43] The BSI is the domestic equivalent to a theater base in other areas of responsibility (AORs). It may be the aerial port of debarkation and may become the joint reception, staging, onward movement, and integration (JRSOI) facility for the joint forces. The USNORTHCOM or USPACOM commander designates the BSI after receiving concurrence of the owning military department Secretary. Not all states have a DOD facility capable of handling military or heavy commercial aircraft. Units need to be prepared to conduct JRSOI from a civilian aerial port of debarkation and conduct further movement to a BSI or incident area.

- ○ **Joint Reception, Staging, Onward movement, and Integration.** The essential process that assembles deploying forces, consisting of personnel, equipment, and materiel arriving in theater, into forces capable of meeting the CCDR's operational requirement.[44] During JRSOI, responsibilities are delineated, communications frequencies are deconflicted, and incoming personnel are fed and housed prior to departure to forward areas. JRSOI is vital to the success of the mission. The reception process varies by mission but always has accountability for personnel and equipment as key concerns. Various briefings

---

[43] JP 3-27, *Homeland Defense,* 12 July 2007.
[44] Ibid.

such as a local area orientation, safety, communications, and logistics support may be provided. Personnel should also be briefed on chain of command, ROE/RUF, and any legal restrictions to operations.

STATE PREPARATIONS

A domestic incident always begins and ends local with local resources being used, and elevates when non-federal resources have been exhausted. As such, the initial incident commander is normally a leader from the first responder organizations, and may be from the local law enforcement or fire department. When the problem cannot be controlled at the local level, the state government will get involved with its resources.

Each state has an agency comparable to FEMA designed to direct a response. During an incident, the C2 function is run by the state's emergency operations center, led by the Governor. A parallel structure to the State Government is the National Guard's JOC, within the state's Joint Force Headquarters (JFHQ). It is led by the TAG, who reports to the Governor. This provides a close connection between the state's political and National Guard leadership. Other state agencies, including law enforcement and natural resource management could also become involved. Other members of the emergency operations center/JOC include the NRF emergency support and joint staff functions.

At the JOC, the ANG determines its current capabilities based on its inventory of personnel and equipment, and categorizes that capability by FEMA NRF emergency support function. Based on the National Guard Empowerment Act of 2008 and the ANG Domestic Operations Equipment Requirements process, the ANG identifies "non-standard" equipment requirements for domestic responses. Also, each JOC should have a thorough understanding of local agencies, their capabilities and limitations, and any local factors (terrain, weather, legal issues, etc.) that may impact their ability to respond. Therefore, the JOC should serve as the focal point for local preparation and any later federal involvement. Installation commanders should interact with their respective JOC to ensure proper local planning and any response actions are coordinated.

REGIONAL PREPARATIONS

Requests for state support should be made to the state coordination officer (SCO) typically at the state EOC. The SCO will coordinate with state agencies to determine which agency is best to respond to a request. As mentioned above at the state level, EMACs can exist across all States. For example, there is a limited number of States which have C-130 aircraft equipped for airborne firefighting operations, but several states call on this capability periodically. Other examples include expeditionary medical support (EMEDS) which has a basic capability in every state, but the larger EMEDS bedded hospitals reside for ANG use on the east coast (Pennsylvania), central plains (Kansas) and west coast (Washington) to support the entire national system.

EMAC covers a wide range of disciplines to include law enforcement, legal, fire, EMS, and ANG capabilities.

FEMA's guidance from the President is to create a response system that "stabilizes an event within 72 hours."

FEDERAL PREPARATIONS

According to Executive Order (EO) 12656, "[e]ffective national security emergency preparedness planning requires the identification of functions that would have to be performed during such an emergency, the assignment of responsibility for developing of plans for performing these functions, and the assignment of responsibility for developing the capability to implement those plans." The primary agency involved in almost all domestic incidents is DHS. Within this department resides a widely known relief organization within the United States, FEMA.

Airborne firefighting assets may be required anywhere in the country, but are only maintained by a handful of units.

Presidential Policy Directive-8 is aimed at strengthening the security and resilience of the United States through systematic preparation for the threats that pose the greatest risk to the security of the Nation, including acts of terrorism, cyber attacks, pandemics, and catastrophic natural disasters. National preparedness is the shared responsibility of all levels of government, the private and nonprofit sectors, and individual citizens. Everyone can contribute to safeguarding the Nation from harm. As such, while this directive is intended to galvanize action by the federal government, it is also aimed at facilitating an integrated, all-of-Nation, capabilities-based approach to preparedness.

The National Response Framework (NRF) and annexes outline which agency will take the lead for various events, and how the leadership transition from one agency to the other takes place. FEMA also has standing plans which identify expected support from the DOD. These support requirements are pre-identified and prioritized, which aids planning, training, and actual response efforts.

The air component staff should work with FEMA and the related DCO, DCE, and EPLO to ensure proper integration of Air Force capabilities into response plans. "The air component staff should work with FEMA and related state JOCs to ensure proper integration of Air Force capabilities into response plans. Staff members should work with the states to develop disaster plans, identify shortfalls, and gain clearer understanding of capabilities across all levels of government."

One critical task is planning to assist in the continuity of government at the federal level. The Air Force currently has plans for continuity of operations (COOP) and has a significant input into the threat assessment process.

DOD-level policies mandate that COOP plans are developed and maintained to ensure essential functions continue unabated during national emergencies. These plans integrate with, and are required to support, overarching and enduring constitutional government, continuity of the presidency, and continuity of government programs. Current guidelines require an "all hazards" approach to continuity planning covering any contingency, from natural or man-made disasters to a general nuclear war. COOP plans support continuity of government (COG) and enduring Constitutional government programs.

Historical events indicate the disruption of Air Force operations is a distinct possibility. Survival of the Air Force is critical to the defense of the nation. As such it is crucial that each echelon of the Air Force understand its role in supporting Air Force mission essential functions. All Airmen should be prepared and know what actions to take when COOP is implemented.

Headquarters Air Force, major commands, direct reporting units, and field operating agencies should possess a comprehensive and effective COOP program.[45] All Air Force organizations should develop plans to ensure continuity of its essential functions, including alert and notification of personnel, movement of key people, and operational capability. COOP planning is best maintained by developing an integrated plan and solution among all efforts that ensure continuity of missions. These efforts include force protection, information assurance, counterterrorism, antiterrorism, mission assurance, critical infrastructure protection, and others.

Presidential Executive Order 12656, Section 202, *Continuity of Government,* states, in pertinent part: "The head of each Federal department and agency shall ensure the continuity of essential functions in any national security emergency by providing for: succession to office and emergency delegation of authority." The DOD develops plans and policies to support the continuity of government functions. Various Air Force organizations may be called upon to support COG planning and execution initiatives.

---

[45] AFI 10-208, *Air Force Continuity of Operations (COOP) Program*, provides guidance for developing programs to ensure continuity of essential operations of the Air Force during an impending or actual national emergency.

CONCLUSION

This doctrine document describes the scope of homeland operations, including the role of the COMAFFOR in planning and execution. Commanders at all levels should understand the legal guidelines and limitations for supporting these operations. The safety and security of the American people is the primary concern. To that end, Airmen of any specialty may be called upon and should understand how they would be employed within the homeland.

Since the Air Force is heavily reliant on the Guard and Reserve components, the COMAFFOR and staff should understand how to use forces in either Title 10 or Title 32 status. Plans should account for the possibility of a dual status commander, as well as how to interact with other civilian agencies. Perhaps most importantly, the COMAFFOR should ensure that no Airman, regardless of status, is left geographically or administratively stranded. A clear line of authority should exist so that leaders at every level, from theater down to line supervisors, can properly lead, direct, and care for those responding to an event.

By forging command lines and establishing interagency relationships in times of peace, the Air Force will be able to respond quickly, efficiently, and effectively in times of crisis.

AT THE VERY HEART OF WARFARE LIES DOCTRINE...

APPENDIX A

NATIONAL POLICY AND LAW

The Air Force carefully examines US policy, domestic law, and international obligations, applicable, when planning homeland operations. There are two general points regarding homeland operations and the law.

First is the overall legal framework affecting the application of airpower in the homeland. There are restrictions on using the military to collect intelligence in the homeland. In addition, there are restrictions on using the military for direct law enforcement duties in the civilian community, with exceptions. Some examples include the President's ability to invoke the Insurrection Act if needed and legislation permitting some use of the military in direct law enforcement roles to counter the influx of illegal narcotics.

Second is the law and its impact on potential financial reimbursement to the DOD. When managing the consequences of an event, the states normally exercise primacy over domestic incidents. Only when they ask for federal assistance, or in extraordinary circumstances, does the federal government get involved. The request process is key for the military because except for immediate emergency situations, a formal request by the state followed by Presidential approval is necessary for the military Services to get financially reimbursed. More information can be found in the Stafford Act (42 U.S.C. §§ 5121 *et seq.*).

Because of the legal and policy complexities, prompt and frequent consultations with military legal experts are among the most important considerations in planning for and employing military assets. The homeland legal environment is very complex and dynamic. Legal experts can help. The following is a nonexclusive list of legal sources for homeland operations.

Anti-Deficiency Act (ADA), 31 U.S.C. §§ 1341-42, 1511-19: This act generally prohibits the obligation or expenditure of appropriated funds in advance of, or in excess of, an appropriation by Congress.

Defense Against Weapons of Mass Destruction (WMD) Act, 50 U.S.C. §§ 2301-2367: Requires DOD coordination with WMD response agencies. Authorizes DOD support to DOJ when the SecDef and Attorney General jointly determine that a WMD threat exists and civil authorities lack sufficient capabilities.

Economy Act, 31 U.S.C. § 1535: This act governs transfer of material between executive branch agencies within the federal government. The Economy Act does not apply to the transfer of material to non-federal law enforcement agencies (LEAs). Reimbursement to the DOD from civilian law enforcement agencies is authorized under 10 U.S.C. § 377 to the extent such would be authorized under The Economy Act.

Insurrrection Act, 10 U.S.C. §§ 331-335: These statutes authorize the use of military forces by presidential order in response to civil disturbances, including rebellion, insurgency, insurrection, or domestic violence such that the state authorities cannot or will not enforce state or federal law. The statutes permit the President to use federal forces in response to a request from a state or territory, to enforce federal authority, or to protect Constitutional rights. (See DODD 3025.12, *Military Assistance with Civil Disturbances.*)

Executive Order 12656, Assignment of Emergency Preparedness Responsibilities: The national security emergency preparedness policy of the US is to have sufficient capabilities at all levels of government to meet essential defense and civilian needs during any national security emergency. A national security emergency is any occurrence, including natural disaster, military attack, terrorist attack, technological emergency, or other emergency that seriously degrades or seriously threatens the national security of the US.

Executive Order 13228, Establishing the Office of Homeland Security and the Homeland Security Council: The Office of Homeland Security is headed by the Assistant to the President for Homeland Security. Its mission is to develop and coordinate the implementation of a comprehensive national strategy to secure the US from terrorist threats or attacks. The office coordinates the executive branch's efforts to detect, prepare for, prevent, protect against, respond to, and recover from terrorist attack within the US.

Foreign Intelligence Surveillance Act (FISA) of 1978 and Amendments, 50 U.S.C. §§ 1801 *et seq.*: FISA establishes a legal framework for foreign intelligence surveillance separate from ordinary law enforcement surveillance. It is aimed at regulating the collection of foreign intelligence information in furtherance of US counterintelligence, while protecting the privacy interests of US citizens. Under FISA, surveillance is generally permitted based on a finding of probable cause that the surveillance target is a foreign power or an agent of a foreign power; in these cases, specific procedural processes must be adhered to.

Homeland Security Act (HSA) of 2002, 6 U.S.C. §§ 101 *et seq.*: HSA establishes the Department of Homeland Security by combining and consolidating previously existing agencies, such as the Coast Guard, Transportation Security Administration, Secret Service, Customs, and the Immigration and Naturalization Service, under one department. The DHS mission is to prevent terrorist attacks within the US; reduce the vulnerability of the US to terrorism; and minimize the damage, and assist in the recovery, from terrorist attacks that occur within the US. DHS also has responsibility for investigating and prosecuting terrorism.

Military Cooperation With Civilian Law Enforcement Officials, 10 U.S.C. §§ 371-382: These sections authorize support to civilian LEA and deal with the use of military information, equipment, facilities, and personnel.

Military Information: Information collected during the normal course of military operations may be forwarded to federal, state, or local LEA if the information is relevant to a violation of criminal law. While the needs of the LEA may be considered when scheduling routine missions, missions may not be planned for the primary purpose of aiding LEA. (See DODD 5525.5, *DOD Cooperation with Civilian Law Enforcement Officials.*)

Intelligence: The USA Patriot Act removed some of the legal obstacles to the sharing of information between law enforcement and intelligence components. Intelligence is a specialized activity that is governed by multiple Congressional statutes, Executive Orders (EO), and DOD Directives. (See EO 12333, *United States Intelligence Activities*; DODD 5240.1, *DOD Intelligence Activities*; DOD 5440.1-R, *Procedures Governing the Activities of DOD Intelligence Components that Affect United States Persons*; and AFI 14-104, *Oversight of Intelligence Activities.*)

Military Equipment and Facilities: Military equipment and facilities may be made available to LEAs, subject to certain restrictions. (See DODD 5525.5, *DOD Cooperation with Civilian Law Enforcement Officials*) Generally, military working dogs can be used to support civilian LEAs. (See AFI 31-121, *Military Working Dog Program.*)

Military Personnel: Except when authorized by statute or the Constitution, direct participation by military personnel in the execution or enforcement of the law is prohibited. Prohibited activities include interdiction, searches and seizures, arrests, and surveillance activities. Generally, the Air Force will not provide advanced military training to civilian law enforcement agencies. Permissible training includes basic marksmanship, patrolling, mission planning, medical, and survival skills. (See DODD 5525.5, *DOD Cooperation with Civilian Law Enforcement Officials.*)

National Defense Authorization Acts: Since 1991, Congress has annually renewed military support for counterdrug operations. Under this, the SecDef may authorize support to federal, state, local, or foreign LEAs if requested. Types of support include maintenance and repair of DOD equipment, transportation of personnel and supplies for the purpose of facilitating counterdrug activities, counterdrug training activities, and aerial and ground reconnaissance, and provision of support for command and control networks. 10 U.S.C. § 124 makes the DOD the lead federal agency for the detection and monitoring of aerial and maritime transit of illegal drugs into the US. 32 U.S.C. § 112 authorizes certain federal funding for the state counterdrug activities of the National Guard.

National Emergencies Act, 50 U.S.C. §§ 1601-1651: This act establishes a process for presidential declarations of emergencies. These declarations must be published in the Federal Register and Congress must review declarations every six months.

Congress is also able to terminate these declarations. This act does not impact the President's Constitutional authority.

Posse Comitatus Act (PCA), 18 U.S.C. § 1385: The PCA prohibits the use of the Army or the Air Force for law enforcement purposes, except as authorized by Congress and the United States Constitution. This prohibition applies to Navy and Marine Corps personnel as a matter of DOD policy. Prohibited direct support includes arrests, searches, and seizures as well as subjecting civilians to compulsory, prescriptive military service. The PCA does not apply to National Guard units in non-federal status.

> Military Purpose: The PCA does not prohibit direct support to law enforcement agencies if the primary purpose is to further a military or foreign affairs function of the US. Actions that serve a primarily military purpose include investigations taken pursuant to the Uniform Code of Military Justice or other military administrative proceedings, and actions taken pursuant to a commander's inherent authority to protect military personnel, property, or guests, or to maintain order on an installation.

> Emergency Authority: The PCA does not prohibit direct support in emergency situations when the action is taken under the inherent right of the US to preserve order and carry out government operations. During sudden or unexpected emergencies, responsible DOD officials or commanders may approve the use of military forces in a law enforcement capacity in order to prevent the loss of life or the wanton destruction of property, or to restore governmental functioning or order. This "immediate response" authority should be used with great caution and in extremely unusual situations.

Presidential Policy Directive–8, National Preparedness (PPD-8): PPD-8 is aimed at "strengthening the security and resilience" of the U.S. through "systematic preparation for the threats that pose the greatest risk to the security of the Nation."

Robert T. Stafford Disaster Relief and Emergency Assistance Act, 42 U.S.C. §§ 5121 *et seq.* [Stafford Act]: The statutory authority for federal disaster assistance. The Act provides procedures for declaring an emergency or major disaster, as well as the type and amount of federal assistance available. The Act authorizes the President to provide DOD assets for relief once a disaster is declared. After a presidential determination is made, DOD may use resources to "save lives, protect property," and avert future threats (see DODD 3025.18, *Defense Support of Civil Authorities*).

Mobilization of Reserve Component Forces: There are several authorities that could be used to involuntarily call Reserve Component Forces to active duty.[46] These authorities are hierarchical with longer periods of involuntary active duty and higher level declarations required as the severity of the situation increases. The most dire Homeland Defense scenario would likely result in a congressionally declared war or

---

[46] The various Manpower Mobilization Options are discussed in greater detail in chapter IV of JP 4-05, Joint Mobilization Planning.

national emergency which would authorize recalling reserve components under 10 USC 12301(a) for the duration of the war or emergency plus 6 months. Upon a presidential declaration of national emergency, 10 USC 12302 authorizes involuntary mobilization for the reserve for up to 24 consecutive months. If the Homeland Defense response gives rise to a contingency operation for which the president determines an augmentation of the active force is required then 10 USC 12304 could be used for calling reservists to duty for up to 365 days. Homeland Support requirements are also addressed in 10 USC 12304. Specifically, its authority may be used to respond to the use or threatened us of a WMD or an actual or threatened terrorist attack upon the United States that could result in a significant loss of life or property. However, 10 USC 12304 specifically may not be used to respond to a serious natural or manmade disaster, accident, or catastrophe. Responses for those events are authorized under 10 USC 12304a which permits the Secretary of Defense upon the request of a governor to call Service Reserve (but not ANG) forces to involuntary active duty for up to 120 days. It is anticipated that ANG response to such events will be under state or other federal authority. Notwithstanding, the variety of involuntary methods, volunteerism under 10 USC 12301(d) is available for all Homeland Defense and Homeland Support responses for which use of the Armed Forces is authorized.[47]

Title 32, U.S. Code: This Act establishes authorities for a National Guard member to function under the command of a state governor while relying on the use of federal funding.

---

[47] The various Manpower Mobilization Options are discussed in greater detail in chapter IV of JP 4-05, Joint Mobilization Planning.

APPENDIX B

NOTIONAL SEQUENCE OF EVENTS FOR DEFENSE SUPPORT OF CIVIL AUTHORITIES

- ✪ Ongoing emergency preparedness actions take place day-to-day (e.g., Air Force weather forces monitoring hurricane status). EPLOs plan with state and regional agencies.

- ✪ Emergency event occurs—may be natural or man-made.

- ✪ Local responders converge at disaster scene and take command of response.

- ✪ DHS and DOD (JDOMS) become aware of the event and begin planning in case called upon to respond; AFNORTH and PACAF (as applicable), the Air Force Operations Center, and AFNSEP also become aware of the emergency.

- ✪ If disaster is potentially man-made and a crime may have been committed, then DOJ may begin planning.

- ✪ Local responders recognize scope of event is beyond their capability and the state government becomes involved.

- ✪ DHS, DOD, and DOJ (if appropriate) may send liaison officers to the scene to advise the on-scene officers and prepare for federal response if needed.

- ✪ AFNSEP may source Air Force EPLOs to state(s) as advisors.

- ✪ State authorities recognize scope of event is beyond their capability and request federal assistance through proper authorities (e.g., NORTHCOM CDR, SECDEF, POTUS, etc., depending on the event).

- ✪ A presidential declaration is made; specific involvement of federal agencies is approved.

- ✪ DHS assigns an FCO.

- ✪ DOD through USNORTHCOM/USPACOM activates the DCO.

- ✪ DHS/FEMA will request DOD support through the RFA process. Once the RFA is validated by the DCO and reviewed by CCDR, DOD forces are sourced and approved through JDOMS by the SecDef.

✪ If Air Force forces are tasked to assist, every effort should be made to present these forces as an AETF through a COMAFFOR to the JTF commander. The COMAFFOR should be given OPCON of Air Force forces.

✪ Once a RFA/MA is complete and the LFA no longer needs the capability, the DCO should notify the CCDR and coordinate with the air component to release AF forces.

REFERENCES

Air Force Publications

All AFDDs and AFIs are available at http://www.e-publishing.af.mil/. AFDDs are also available at http://www.au.af.mil/au/lemay/main.htm .

Joint Publications

All JPs are available at https://jdeis.js.mil/jdeis/index.jsp?pindex=21.

Other Publications

Department of Defense Directive (DODD) 3025.12. *Military Assistance for Civil Disturbances (MACDIS),* 4 February 1994.

Department of Homeland Security, *National Incident Management System*, December 2008.

DODD 3025.18. *Defense Support of Civil Authorities (DSCA),* 29 December 2010.

DODD 5525.5, *DOD Cooperation with Civilian Law Enforcement Officials,* Change 1, 20 December 1989.

Foreign Intelligence Surveillance Act of 1978, as amended, 50 U.S.C. §§ 1801 *et seq*.

Homeland Security Council. *National Strategy for Homeland Security.* Washington, D.C.: October 2007.

Homeland Security Presidential Directive-Five. Management of Domestic Incidents, 28 February 2003.

National Guard Instruction 500-1/Air National Guard Instruction 10-8101, *National Guard Domestic Operations,* 13 June 2008.

National Security Strategy, May 2010.

US Department of Homeland Security. *National Response Framework.* Washington, D.C.: January 2008.

US Department of Homeland Security, *National Search and Rescue Plan of the United States.* Washington, D.C.: United States Coast Guard, 2007.

GLOSSARY

Abbreviations and Acronyms

ACA	airspace control authority
ADCON	administrative control
AETF	air expeditionary task force
AFAux	Air Force Auxiliary
AFDD	Air Force doctrine document
AFI	Air Force instruction
AFIMS	Air Force Incident Management System
AFNORTH	Air Forces Northern
AFNSEP	Air Force National Security and Emergency Preparedness Agency
AFOSI	Air Force Office of Special Investigations
AFRCC	Air Force Rescue Coordination Center
AFTRANS	Air Forces Transportation
AMC	Air Mobility Command
ANG	Air National Guard
ANR	Alaska NORAD Region
AOC	air operations center
AOR	area of responsibility
BSI	base support installation
C2	command and control
CANR	Canadian NORAD region
CAP	Civil Air Patrol
CBRN	chemical, biological, radiological, and nuclear
CCDR	combatant commander
CDRUSNORTHCOM	Commander, United States Northern Command
CDRUSPACOM	Commander, United States Pacific Command
CDRUSSOCOM	Commander, United States Special Operations Command
COCOM	combatant command (authority)
COG	continuity of government
COMAFFOR	commander, Air Force forces
CONR	continental NORAD Region
CONUS	continental United States
COOP	continuity of operations
DCA	defensive counterair
DCO	defense coordination officer
DHS	Department of Homeland Security
DIRLAUTH	direct liaison authorized
DOD	Department of Defense

DODD	Department of Defense Directive
DOJ	Department of Justice
DSCA	defense support of civil activities
EMAC	emergency management assistance compact
EMEDS	expeditionary medical support
EO	executive order
EOC	emergency operations center
EOD	explosive ordnance disposal
EP	emergency preparedness
EPLO	emergency preparedness liaison officer
EXORD	execution order
FAA	Federal Aviation Administration
FBI	Federal Bureau of Investigations
FCO	federal coordinating officer
FEMA	Federal Emergency Management Agency
FISA	Foreign Intelligence Surveillance Act
FTSF	Federal Team Staging Facility
GCC	geographic combatant commander
HD	homeland defense
HSA	Homeland Security Act
HSPD	homeland security presidential directive
JDOMS	Joint Director of Military Support
JFACC	joint force air component commander
JFC	joint force commander
JFHQ-State	joint force headquarters-state
JOC	joint operations center
JRSOI	joint reception, staging, onward movement, and integration
JTF	joint task force
JTF-AK	Joint Task Force-Alaska
LEA	law enforcement agency
LFA	lead federal agency
MACDIS	military assistance to civil disturbances
MOA	memorandum of agreement
MOU	memorandum of understanding
MSLE	military support of law enforcement
NG	National Guard
NGB	National Guard Bureau

NGCC	National Guard Coordination Center
NIMS	National Incident Management System
NORAD	North American Aerospace Defense Command
NRF	national response framework
NRP	National Response Plan
NSHS	National Strategy for Homeland Security
NSSE	national special security events
OPCON	operational control
PACAF	Pacific Air Forces
PCA	Posse Comitatus Act
ROE	rules of engagement
ROMO	range of military operations
RUF	rules for the use of force
SAD	State Active Duty
SAR	search and rescue
SECAF	Secretary of the Air Force
SecDef	Secretary of Defense
TAG	the adjutant general
UCP	Unified Command Plan
USC	United States code
USNORTHCOM	United States Northern Command
USPACOM	United States Pacific Command
USTRANSCOM	United States Transportation Command
USSOCOM	United States Special Operations Command
USSTRATCOM	United States Strategic Command
WMD	weapons of mass destruction

Definitions

air sovereignty. A nation's inherent right to exercise absolute control and authority over the airspace above its territory. (JP 1-02)

continuity of operations. The degree or state of being continuous in the conduct of functions, tasks, or duties necessary to accomplish a military action or mission in carrying out the national military strategy. (JP 3-0)

homeland. The physical region that includes the continental United States, Alaska, Hawaii, United States possessions and territories, and surrounding territorial waters and airspace. (JP 3-28)

homeland defense. The protection of United States sovereignty, territory, domestic population, and critical defense infrastructure against external threats and aggression or other threats as directed by the President. Also called **HD**. (JP 3-27)

homeland security. A concerted national effort to prevent terrorist attacks within the United States; reduce America's vulnerability to terrorism, major disasters, and other emergencies; and minimize the damage and recover from attacks, major disasters, and other emergencies that occur. Also called **HS**. (JP 3-28)